Skills Builders

YEAR 3

GRAMMAR AND PUNCTUATION

Nicola Morris

Acknowledgements

Every effort has been made to trace all copyright holders, but if any have been inadvertently overlooked, the Publishers will be pleased to make the necessary arrangements at the first opportunity.

Although every effort has been made to ensure that website addresses are correct at time of going to press, Rising Stars cannot be held responsible for the content of any website mentioned in this book. It is sometimes possible to find a relocated web page by typing in the address of the home page for a website in the URL window of your browser.

Hachette UK's policy is to use papers that are natural, renewable and recyclable products and made from wood grown in sustainable forests. The logging and manufacturing processes are expected to conform to the environmental regulations of the country of origin.

ISBN: 978-1-78339-707-5

Text, design and layout © 2016 Rising Stars UK Ltd

First published in 2016 by Rising Stars UK Ltd
Rising Stars UK Ltd, An Hachette UK Company
Carmelite House
50 Victoria Embankment
London EC4Y 0DZ

www.risingstars-uk.com

All facts are correct at time of going to press.

Author: Nicola Morris
Educational Consultant: Madeleine Barnes
Publisher: Laura White
Illustrator: Emily Skinner
Logo design: Amparo Barrera, Kneath Associates Ltd
Design: Julie Martin
Typesetting: Newgen
Cover design: Amparo Barrera, Kneath Associates Ltd
Project Manager: Sarah Bishop, Out of House Publishing
Copy Editor: Hayley Fairhead
Proofreader: Jennie Clifford
Software development: Alex Morris
Photo © imageBROKER / Alamy Stock Photo

British Library Cataloguing-in-Publication Data
A CIP record for this book is available from the British Library.
Printed by Liberduplex S.L., Barcelona, Spain

Contents

All of the answers can be found online. To get access, simply register or login at **www.risingstars-uk.com**.

1 Sentence punctuation

Sentences begin with a **capital letter** and end with a **full stop (.)**.
If the sentence is a question, it ends with a **question mark (?)**.

Where is your jumper?

If it is an exclamation, it ends with an **exclamation mark (!)**.

What a great film!

Activity 1

Rewrite these sentences with the correct punctuation.

.	ABC	?	!

a) What time is it

b) my favourite sport is swimming

c) Stop doing that

d) who is coming with me

e) come here now

f) I had pasta for my tea

Activity 2

Write a sentence about yourself using correct punctuation.

_____

_____

Write a question for your friend using correct punctuation.

_____

_____

2 Commas in a list

When we write a list, we separate each item with a **comma (,)**.
The final two items are separated using **and**.

I bought apples, bananas, apricots, grapes **and** peaches.

We can write a list of **adjectives** to describe someone
or something. Each **adjective** is separated with a **comma**.

The ancient, dark, deserted city.

Activity 1

Add **commas** in the correct places in each sentence below.

a) My pencil case is full of pens pencils and felt-tips.

b) Ali's favourite colours are green yellow and orange.

c) Amy made a cake with flour milk eggs and butter.

d) I went to the zoo to see elephants gorillas giraffes crocodiles and penguins.

e) Everton Liverpool Manchester United Chelsea and West Ham are playing in the FA Cup.

Activity 2

Choose your own **adjectives** to describe each person or thing. Put the **commas** in the correct places.

a) the _____ _____ baby

b) a _____ _____ village

c) our _____ _____ _____ house

d) the _____ _____ _____ car

Use these pictures to write a sentence about what you bought at the shop.

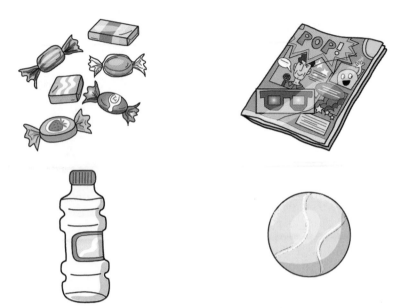

Use these pictures to write a sentence about what sports you like playing.

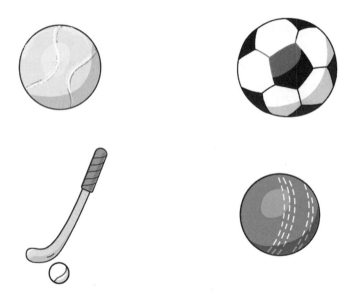

Investigate!

Can you write a list of **adjectives** to describe this robot?
Put them into a sentence and remember the **commas**!

3 Apostrophes

We use an **apostrophe** to show **contraction** and **possession**.

- **Contraction** is when letters are missing.

  he will ⟶ he'll, cannot ⟶ can't

- **Possession** is when someone owns something.

  Danielle's bag, the **rabbit's** hutch

Activity 1

Why is an **apostrophe** used in these words?

Holly's football   the cat's collar   the queen's throne

An apostrophe is used to show _____.

Why is an **apostrophe** used in these words?

I'm   didn't   they'll

An apostrophe is used to show _____.

Activity 2

Add an **apostrophe** in the correct place in each sentence below.

a) Im going to the shops after school.

b) Everyone was looking forward to Anyas party.

c) They didnt know where to go.

d) He wont mind if you borrow his book.

e) Zainabs handwriting was very neat.

f) Youll need to wash the dogs bowl before you go out.

4 Nouns, verbs and adjectives

Sentences contain different word classes, which have different jobs.

- **Nouns** are naming words.
- **Verbs** are action or being words (**jumping**, **am**).
- **Adjectives** are describing words (**tiny**, **delicious**).

There are two types of nouns.

- **Common nouns** name a person, place or thing.
  a girl, **an apple**
- **Proper nouns** are used for people's names, titles, place names or days of the week.
  The Gruffalo, **Monday**, **London**

Activity 1

Copy the table into your book and sort these words into **common nouns** and **proper nouns**.

Common nouns	Proper nouns

London   homework   crocodile   December   *The Lion King*
rollercoaster   Alton Towers   violin   boat   Thursday
house   television   Saskia   country   *Fantastic Mr Fox*

Activity 2

Identify and write down the **verb** in each of these sentences.

a) Ahmed wrote a letter.

b) The children went to the zoo.

c) Everyone sang 'Happy Birthday'.

d) The baby slept all night.

e) She was here.

Activity 3

Identify and write down the **adjectives** in each of these sentences. There could be more than one!

a) The orange was juicy.

b) Last night, we went to a fantastic party.

c) The rain poured from the dark sky.

d) It was a majestic, ancient castle.

e) A small boat sailed across the peaceful lake.

Activity 4

Choose your own **noun, verb** or **adjective** to complete each sentence.

a) The _____ sat on the wall.

b) She was happy to receive a _____ present.

c) The little girl _____ across the room.

d) At last, the visitor _____.

e) My favourite film is _____.

Investigate!

Make a list of **nouns, adjectives** and **verbs**. Put them together in different ways to create different sentences – some of them may be silly sentences!

5 Singular and plural

Remember the rules for making **plurals**.

- For most words, just add **s**.

  coat ⟶ coats

- For words that end **ss**, **sh**, **ch** or **x**, add **es**.

  witch ⟶ witches, fox ⟶ foxes

- For words that end in **y**, change **y** to **i** before adding **es**, unless there's a vowel before the **y**.

  lady ⟶ ladies but **trolley ⟶ trolleys**

- For most words that end in **f** or **fe**, change the **f** to **ves**.

  scarf ⟶ scarves

- Some **plurals** are irregular.

  child ⟶ children, foot ⟶ feet

- Sometimes the singular and the plural are the same.

  deer ⟶ deer

Activity 1

Write the **plural** for each **singular noun** given below.

school _____   wish _____   box _____

lorry _____   knife _____   latch _____

sheep _____

Activity 2

Rewrite each sentence so that the **singular noun** is **plural**. Check if you need to change any other words in the sentence so that they make sense.

a) Please put the dish down. _____

b) There was a fly nearby. _____

c) My dog was running happily. _____

d) She built a new shelf. _____

6 Expanded noun phrases

An **expanded noun phrase** gives more detail about the noun. They make your writing more interesting and help the reader to build up a picture in their mind.

There are two ways to create an **expanded noun phrase**.

- We can add **adjectives** to the **noun**.

  The fast, shiny, red car.

- We can add information about the **noun**.

  The bird is in the tree.

Activity 1

Add an **adjective** to the following sentences to create an **expanded noun phrase**.

a) The _____ horse galloped away.

b) It was a _____ night.

c) The _____ star twinkled.

d) They ate a _____ meal.

Activity 2

Choose a word or phrase from each column to create as many different **expanded noun phrases** as you can. One has been done for you.

a young elephant next to the pond

Determiner	Adjective	Noun	Additional information
a	tall	elephant	on the hill
an	young	friend	next to the pond
the	loud	ice-cream	in my hand
	delicious	tree	far away
	orange	helicopter	at the bus stop
	huge	ball	in the sunshine

Investigate!

Add your own ideas to each list in Activity 2 to make up some more **expanded noun phrases**.

11

7 Simple sentences

Words are joined together to make **clauses**. A **clause** has one idea or event. It has a **verb** and a **noun**. Simple sentences can have just one **clause**.

The girl walked to school.

More information can be added.

The little girl walked to school.
The girl walked to school slowly.
The girl walked to school over the hill.

Activity 1

Put each set of words in the correct order to make a **simple sentence**. Remember to add a full stop at the end of each sentence.

a) barked The dog _____

b) fell Rob over _____

c) drove We the car in _____

d) the shop to walked Charlie _____

e) lifted elephant The his trunk huge _____

f) sunny was Today a very day _____

Remember!

A sentence has to begin with a **capital letter** and end with a **full stop**. A sentence has to make sense. If your sentence doesn't make sense, you know that something is missing or in the wrong place.

Activity 2

Add words in the spaces to complete these **simple sentences**. You can decide how much information to add, but check that each sentence makes sense.

a) The man _____.

b) A _____ sparkled.

c) The huge _____ roared.

d) All of the _____.

e) Our friends _____.

Activity 3

How many **clauses** do these **sentences** have?

a) The cat drank its milk.

b) The girl opened the door and she entered the house.

c) He sat on the comfortable chair.

d) Five birds flew into the sky.

e) Ala wanted an ice lolly but the shop had run out.

Investigate!

How many sentences can you make that contain only three words?

The boy danced.

The sun shone.

8 Sentence types

There are four different types of sentence.

- A **statement** tells you something, and ends with a **full stop**.

  My favourite colour is purple**.**

- A **question** asks you something, and ends with a **question mark**.

  What is your favourite colour**?**

- An **exclamation** makes a statement with emotion, and ends with an **exclamation mark**.

  What a great trip**!**

- A **command** gives an order and can end with a **full stop** or an **exclamation mark**, depending on how it is said.

  Please fill the water bottles**.**

  Fill the water bottles**!**

Activity 1

Label the sentence types below. Write **S** for **statement**, **Q** for **question**, **E** for **exclamation** or **C** for **command**.

a) When are you going on holiday? _____   d) Who is next? _____

b) There are 30 children in the class. _____   e) What a dangerous thing to do! _____

c) Close the door behind you. _____

Activity 2

Change these **questions** into **statements**.

Would you like a cake? I would like a cake.

a) Is it sunny today?   c) Can you come to my house?

b) Are you going to read a book?   d) Should we meet at 8 o'clock?

Activity 3

a) Write a **question** where the answer will be 'yes'.

_____

b) Write a **question** where the answer will be 'no'.

_____

c) Write a **question** that cannot be answered with 'yes' or 'no'.

_____

d) Write an **exclamation** sentence about something you really like.

_____

e) Write an **exclamation** sentence about something you really don't like.

_____

f) Write a **command** for someone in your class.

_____

g) Write a **statement** about yourself.

_____

Investigate!

Pick out sentences written in books, newspapers and magazines. Decide whether they are **statements**, **questions**, **exclamations** or **commands**.

15

9 Joining sentences: or, and, but, so

A **conjunction** is a word that is used to join sentences; **or**, **and**, **but** and **so** are conjunctions.

I like bananas **and** I like apples.
The children wanted to go outside **but** it was raining.
Do you want the blue ball **or** would you prefer the red one?
It's sunny outside **so** we're going out to play.

Activity 1

Choose the correct **conjunction** to fit each of these sentences.

or   and   but   so

a) We could watch a film _____ we could play a game.

b) Louisa wanted to go to the party _____ she was ill.

c) I drew my picture carefully _____ then I cut it out.

d) We've got the day off school _____ we can go to the park.

e) Sarim enjoys playing football _____ he likes rounders _____ he's not so keen on rugby.

Activity 2

Choose whether **or** or **and** should join these sentences. Rewrite them to create one sentence.

a) I may go on holiday to Spain. I may go on holiday to Italy.

_____

b) Marwa walked down the road. She went into a shop.

_____

c) It started to rain. Everyone got wet.

_____

d) Do you want pasta for tea? Would you prefer chips?

_____

Activity 3

Choose whether **but** or **so** should join these sentences. Rewrite them to create one sentence.

a) It's Laura's birthday. She's having a party.

_____

b) We wanted to catch the train. We were too late.

_____

c) Jonathan thought he'd scored a goal. The ball didn't go in the net.

_____

d) Zofia's hair has grown very long. She's going to have it cut.

_____

Activity 4

Choose whether **or, and, but** or **so** should join each pair of sentences. Rewrite them to create one sentence.

a) I really wanted an ice-cream. The shop had sold out.

_____

b) You can write with a pen. You can write with a pencil.

_____

c) Jaideep was feeling unwell. His mum gave him some medicine.

_____

d) Jimmy put on his coat. He went outside.

_____

Investigate!

Which of these **conjunctions** do you use most in your own writing? Try to find examples of sentences that contain each **conjunction**. If you can't find one, try writing new sentences. Look at the sentences in this unit to help you.

or   and   but   so

10 Joining sentences: when, if, that, because

The words **when**, **if**, **that** and **because** are also **conjunctions**. They are used to explain or add information.

Fabian will get his pocket money **when** he cleans the car.

The footballer will play tonight **if** he has recovered from injury.

We are all hopeful **that** his knee will be better.

I went to the dentist **because** I needed a filling.

Activity 1

Choose the correct **conjunction** to fit each of these sentences.

when   if   that   because

a) Helen needed a lift _____ her car had broken down.

b) Let me know _____ you want me to get you some milk.

c) I'll come round _____ I've finished my homework.

d) I didn't know _____ she'd moved house.

e) The balloon burst _____ it landed on a pin.

f) She decided _____ she couldn't watch the film _____ it finished late.

Activity 2

Complete each sentence, thinking about what the **conjunction** is telling you.

a) I can have an ice-cream if _____.

b) Gabriel wasn't allowed out to play because _____.

c) They all cheered when _____.

d) It was a shame that _____.

e) Tell me if _____ because I will need to _____.

11 Past and present tense

Verbs in the **past tense** tell us about things that have already happened.

I **walked** to school.

Verbs in the **present tense** tell us about things that are happening now.

I **walk** to school.

Activity 1

Change these sentences from the **present tense** to the **past tense**.

a) We wait at the bus stop.

_____.

b) I watch a great film.

_____.

c) Everyone sits on the field.

_____.

d) Matthew throws the ball and Max catches it.

_____.

Activity 2

Change these sentences from the **past tense** to the **present tense**.

a) We cleaned the house.

_____.

b) I collected the rubbish.

_____.

c) The hamster ate his food.

_____.

d) The bird flapped his wings and flew into the sky.

_____.

Remember!

When we write, we need to decide which **tense** we should be using, and use it consistently all the way through.

Activity 3

Decide which word is the correct **tense** for each sentence, then rewrite the sentence.

a) Last week, we (wrote/write) a story in class.

b) We (enjoy/enjoyed) building sandcastles when we go to the beach.

c) We (play/played) games on the computer while we waited for Dad.

d) Help me (look/looked) for my phone.

e) Yesterday, I (ate/eat) a huge piece of chocolate cake!

f) A few minutes ago, the teacher (blew/blows) the whistle.

Activity 4

Write your own sentences for each of these **verbs,** using the correct **tense.**

cried   shop   runs   thanked

a) _____

b) _____

c) _____

d) _____

Investigate!

Write three sentences in the **present tense** about what you can see in your classroom right now. Then change each one into the **past tense.**

The teacher **works** with the Blue group.

The teacher **worked** with the Blue group.

12 Progressive form of verbs

The **progressive form** of verbs shows whether the actions are happening now or whether they have happened in the past.

We can show that actions are happening in the **present tense** by using **am/are/is**.

She is making a cake. The action is in progress.

We can show that actions were happening in the **past tense** by using **was/were**.

She was making a cake. The action was in progress.

Activity 1

Write down the two words that make up the **verb** in each sentence.

a) I am washing my hair.

b) The doctor was examining the patient.

c) Ali is singing on the stage.

d) Year 3 were eating their lunch.

e) The troll was sitting under the bridge.

Activity 2

Change each sentence below from the **present progressive tense** into the **past progressive tense**.

a) Liz is playing the violin.

_____

b) The whole class are painting pictures.

_____

c) You are listening to the radio.

_____

d) Hannah is opening the envelope.

_____

13 Present perfect form of verbs

We use the **present perfect form** of verbs to say that an action has happened at some point in the past, but we don't specify when it happened. We can do this by using **have** or **has** as part of the verb.

I **have visited** Canada.

She **has learned** to play the piano.

Activity 1

Complete each sentence by adding **have** or **has**.

a) We _____ eaten at that restaurant.

b) It _____ still not stopped raining.

c) Leon and James _____ finished their homework.

d) Zoe _____ lived in Bristol all of her life.

e) Chan _____ always supported Manchester City.

Activity 2

Rewrite each of these sentences so that the **verb** is in the **present perfect form**. Use the verb given in brackets.

a) My cat (love) _____ _____ her squeaky toy since she was a kitten.

b) They (arrive) _____ _____ at the airport.

c) Talia and Kate (study) _____ _____ French at school.

d) Lenny (sing) _____ _____ for many years.

Remember!

General time expressions such as **always**, **never**, **still**, **already** and **since** can be useful in a **present perfect tense** sentence.

You **have** grown **since** I last saw you.

14 Vowels and consonants

The 26 letters of the alphabet are either **vowels** or **consonants**.
We often use these terms when talking about words and
how they are made up.

Vowels	a e i o u
Consonants	b c d f g h j k l m n p q r s t v w x y z

Activity 1

Write down the **consonants** in each of these words.

a) octagon

b) walk

c) fridge

d) climbing

e) lampshade

Activity 2

The words below have their **vowels** missing. Can you work out what these words
should be?

a) cl_sh

b) cl_b

c) p_nc_l

d) t_bl_

e) sch__l

Investigate!

Collect a list of words and take the **vowels** out. Challenge your friends to work
out what the words are.

23

15 Word families

There are groups of words that are based on the same **root** word but belong to different word classes and mean different things.

Care is the **root** word.

Careful and **careless** are adjectives.

Carer is a noun.

Cared is a verb.

Carefully is an adverb.

Activity 1

Write down which word class the underlined word from each family belongs to.

a) joke   <u>jokingly</u>   joked

b) lone   loneliness   lonely   <u>loner</u>

c) able   unable   <u>ability</u>   disable

d) magic   magician   <u>magical</u>   magically

e) wonder   wonderful   <u>wondered</u>

f) cover   <u>uncover</u>   discovery   discover   uncovered

Activity 2

Choose the correct form from the word family to complete each sentence.

a) She was in trouble because of her bad (behaviour/behave) at school.

b) The car drove (speedy/speedily) down the road.

c) A window was (breakable/broken) by the cricket ball.

d) The wizard (possessive/possessed) magic powers.

e) The box had a (variation/variety) of biscuits inside.

Activity 3

Write sentences using two words from each word family.

a) thanks   thankful   thankless   thanked

_____

_____

b) respect   disrespect   respectful   respected

_____

_____

c) friend   friendly   unfriendly   friendship

_____

_____

d) change   exchange   changeable   changed

_____

_____

e) agree   disagree   agreed   agreement

_____

_____

Investigate!

How many words can you and a partner write down that are part of a word family?

16 Prefixes

Prefixes are used to change the meaning of a word. The **prefixes un**, **in**, **dis** and **mis** all have negative meanings.

able ──────→ **un**able

convenient ──────→ **in**convenient

appear ──────→ **dis**appear

behave ──────→ **mis**behave

Activity 1

Which **prefix** can be added to all of the words in each set?

a) tie   lucky   certain   cover

b) count   read   fortune   calculate

c) agree   connect   obey   like

d) active   capable   attentive   accurate

Activity 2

Choose the word with the correct **prefix** for each of these sentences.

a) Mum was looking for her glasses as she had _____ them.
(misplaced/unplaced)

b) The children were _____ because the party was cancelled.
(inappointed/disappointed)

c) It was _____ that the boy won because everyone knew he had cheated.
(unfair/infair)

d) She was sure there were more tickets than that; she must have _____.
(uncounted/miscounted)

e) It was the most _____ film they had ever seen.
(uncredible/incredible)

f) Everyone knows that it is _____ to steal. (mishonest/dishonest)

Here are some more **prefixes**.

- **anti** means 'against'.

  antifreeze

- **auto** means 'self' or 'own'.

  autograph

- **super** means 'greater'.

  superpower

- **re** means 'again' or 'back'.

  review

Activity 3

Write the correct **prefix** for each of these words.

_____matic   _____natural

_____play   _____septic

Activity 4

Copy the table into your book and sort these words so that they are with the correct **prefix**. Some words can be placed in more than one column of the table.

dis	mis	auto	re

inform   consider   biography   do   qualify   connect

take   mobile   infect   behave

Investigate!

Look back over the words in this unit and choose three to use in your own sentences.

17 Determiners

A **determiner** gives information about which **noun** is being talked about. Examples of **determiners** are **a, an, the, this, those, our, all** and **any**.

The choice of **a** or **an** can be used with any **noun**.

The **determiner a** is used when the **noun** begins with a **consonant** and **an** is used when the **noun** begins with a **vowel**.

a banana, an apple

The **determiner the** is used to identify a particular **noun**.

the boy, the cat

Activity 1

Use the rules to help you to decide whether to use **a** or **an** for each word.

a) _____ book

b) _____ tennis ball

c) _____ umbrella

d) _____ experiment

e) _____ lion

f) _____ adventure

g) _____ exciting adventure

h) _____ fantastic adventure

Activity 2

Choose the correct **determiner** to complete each sentence.

all   that   another   her   our   this

a) She brought _____ bike to school today.

b) The packet was empty as Zahra had eaten _____ of the sandwiches.

c) We drove to the seaside in _____ new car.

d) I'm full up so I won't have _____ potato.

e) _____ chair is broken so sit on _____ chair instead.

Activity 3

Circle the **determiner** or **determiners** in each of these sentences.

a) We're ready to go in the classroom now.

b) Rachel couldn't decide so she bought both cakes.

c) His pencil needs sharpening.

d) Those shoes will go with my school uniform.

e) We left our house and walked along the street until we got to that new shop.

Activity 4

Use a **determiner** to complete each sentence.

a) I am waiting for _____ bus.

b) Soon, we will arrive at _____ house.

c) Elon needs to drink _____ water.

d) I'm still hungry so I'll eat _____ biscuit.

e) I have brought _____ apple for _____ snack.

Investigate!

Write down a sentence telling someone to get you something from the classroom. Use **determiners** so they know exactly where to go and what to get.

Please pass me **a** red pencil from **your** pot.

18 Conjunctions to express time and cause

Conjunctions are used to extend sentences and give extra information. They can be used at the beginning or in the middle of sentences.

The king was happy **when** the knight rescued his daughter.

I need to go to the shop **because** we have run out of milk.

Before we go out, we need to put on our coats.

Activity 1

Choose the correct **conjunction** to complete each of these sentences.

when	before	after	while	so	because

a) Cover the table with newspaper _____ you start painting.

b) Leanne eats a lot of vegetables _____ they are healthy.

c) The boy went to bed _____ he had cleaned his teeth.

d) Sasha wouldn't go in the bathroom _____ the spider was there.

e) Jim did all of his chores _____ he got a reward.

f) The audience clapped _____ the singer finished her song.

Activity 2

Change each sentence so that the **conjunction** is at the beginning.

a) Please get me some milk while you're at the shop.

_____

b) Put on sun cream before you go out in this hot weather.

_____

c) I've had to drive to the supermarket since our local shop closed.

_____

19 Subordinate clauses

A **main clause** is a group of words with a **subject** and a **verb** that can stand on its own, making a **simple sentence**.

The alien landed his spaceship in the middle of the school field.

A **subordinate clause** tells us more about the **main clause**. It cannot stand alone. A **main clause** and a **subordinate clause** go together to make a **complex sentence**.

Conjunctions are used to show where a **subordinate clause** begins.

| when | before | after | while | so | because |

They can be used at the beginning or in the middle of a sentence.

The alien landed his spaceship in the middle of the school field **because** he had run out of fuel.

When he ran out of fuel, the alien landed his spaceship in the middle of the school field.

Activity 1

Write the **conjunction** that is used to give further information in each sentence.

a) Sonny meets his dad at the gate when school has finished.

b) The dentist got his drill because he needed to do a filling.

c) After you've had your tea, you can choose what to watch on television.

d) If you're thirsty, get a drink of water.

Activity 2

Complete the sentences below by choosing the correct ending to match each opening.

Main clause	Subordinate clause
I need to go to the doctor's	when we went to Spain.
It was very hot	so that the area will look colourful.
The builders will start work outside today	before she had her tea.
I have to wait here	because I'm feeling ill.
The gardener is planting flowers	until everyone else is ready.
Lottie went to the park	if it doesn't rain.

Activity 3

Circle the **subordinate clause** in each sentence.

a) I will wait for you while you put your shoes on.

b) If you want to win a prize, you will have to buy a raffle ticket.

c) The princess screamed when she saw the dragon.

d) I'm watching my favourite film, so please be quiet.

e) Before you do your homework, make sure you have the right equipment.

f) The dog barked because the postman came to the door.

Activity 4

Rewrite and complete each sentence by adding a **main clause**.

a) Before you go to bed, _____.

b) When the whistle goes, _____.

c) _____ because she fell and hurt her knee.

d) _____ if you win the race.

Investigate!

Look at books in the classroom and collect sentences with **subordinate clauses**. They might give you ideas to use in your own writing.

20 Adverbs

The **suffix ly** can be added to the end of some **adjectives** to make **adverbs**.

quick ⟶ **quickly**

Adverbs give more information about the **verb**. **Adverbs** can be used in different places in a sentence.

The fox moved **quickly** across the garden.
The fox moved across the garden **quickly**.
Quickly, the fox moved across the garden.

For most adjectives just add **ly**. For adjectives that end in **y**, change the **y** to **i** and then add **ly**.

steady ⟶ **steadily**

Activity 1

Change these **adjectives** into **adverbs**.

slow → _____

quiet → _____

careful → _____

worried → _____

happy → _____

noisy → _____

Activity 2

Write an **adverb** to complete each sentence.

a) She ate the chocolates _____.

b) The children played _____ in the swimming pool.

c) _____, the mysterious man entered the building.

d) A queue of people waited at the bus stop _____.

e) On the hill, the sheep grazed _____.

21 Adverbs to express time, place and cause

Adverbs give extra information about the verb in a sentence. They can be used to explain how, how often, when, where or why an action happens. They can be used at the beginning, middle or end of sentences. Some adverbs do a similar job to **conjunctions**.

He shouted **loudly**.

I walk to school **every day**.

Today, we have science and PE.

My friends have gone **inside**.

However, I'm feeling better now.

Activity 1

Copy the table into your book and sort the **adverbs** to show which question they answer.

How?	How often?	When?	Where?

upstairs   usually   yesterday   silently   here   always
above   last year   soon   hopefully

Activity 2

Choose the correct **adverb** to complete each of these sentences.

carefully   never   next   therefore   behind   before
long ago   in a few minutes

a) _____, there lived a beautiful princess in a golden palace.

b) The kitten hid _____ the sofa.

c) Harry's car has broken down, _____ he will have to walk.

d) She had _____ been here before.

e) _____, mix the ingredients together _____.

f) We will have to leave _____, _____ the show has ended.

34

Activity 3

Answer each question by identifying the **adverb** in the sentence.

a) The dog sat nearby.

Where did the dog sit?

_____

b) Yesterday, Ian went to a football match.

When did Ian go to a football match?

_____

c) Mum ran quickly because she was late.

How did Mum run?

_____

d) Sometimes, we go to the milkshake bar for a treat.

How often do we go to the milkshake bar?

_____

e) Earlier today, the children had to stop playing outside.

When did the children have to stop playing?

_____

Investigate!

Look at sentences in books and identify **adverbs** that answer the questions below.

- **How?**
- **How often?**
- **When?**
- **Where?**

Write down a list of the **adverbs** you have identified to use in your own writing.

22 Prepositions

A **preposition** links a **noun** or **pronoun** to another word or phrase in a sentence. They can be used to answer the questions when, where and why. You will notice that some **prepositions** have already appeared as **conjunctions** or **adverbs**.

We have been waiting **since** 4 o'clock.
She was sitting **on** the bus.
His umbrella was ruined **because** of the storm.

Activity 1

Complete each sentence with a **preposition** to answer the question **Where?**.

> in   back   through   over   under

a) The bird made its nest _____ the tree.

b) There was a stream running _____ the field.

c) A helicopter flew _____ the buildings.

d) We found the key _____ the chair.

e) He sat at the _____ of the bus.

Activity 2

Complete each sentence with a **preposition** to answer the question **When?**.

> during   after   until   since   before

a) He will do the washing-up _____ we have gone.

b) _____ the firework display, the pets stayed in the house.

c) I need money from the bank _____ I can go to the shop.

d) I haven't eaten _____ breakfast.

e) Wait _____ the green man shows to cross the road safely.

23 Headings and sub-headings

Headings and **sub-headings** help us to organise non-fiction writing so that it is clear to follow.

- A **heading** is the title at the top of a page or section of a book.

- **Sub-headings** are used to break up the information under the heading. The sub-headings will be related to the heading.

Big cats

Big cats are among the most powerful animals in the world. They are all carnivores and have strong sharp claws and well-developed canine teeth. They hunt other animals but have no predators of their own.

Leopards

The leopard is fast and can leap 6m into the air. Leopards are solitary, spending most of their time alone. They are found in parts of Africa, Asia, India and China.

Cheetahs

The cheetah is the fastest land animal. Most cheetahs are found in the eastern and southern parts of Africa.

Lions

A group of lions is called a pride. Lionesses do most of the hunting while the males guard the pride and protect the cubs. Lions are found in Africa and India.

Tigers

The tiger is the largest of the big cats. A tiger's stripes are like fingerprints – the pattern on each is unique. They are found in some African countries, but hunting and habitat loss have reduced their population.

Activity 1

Look at these three **headings** and decide which three **sub-headings** match each one.

London   The Skeleton   Castles

Headings	London	The Skeleton	Castles
Sub-headings			

When were they built?   What to see   Movement   What were they made out of?

What to do   Where to stay   How it supports our bodies

Why were they built?   Bones

Activity 2

Look at these three **headings** and decide which three **sub-headings** match each one.

Ancient Greece   Plants   Volcanoes

Headings	Ancient Greece	Plants	Volcanoes
Sub-headings			

The life cycle of an apple   Eruption   Gods and heroes   The Olympic Games

Mount Vesuvius   Home life   Pollination   Seed dispersal   Lava

Investigate!

Can you find **headings** and **sub-headings** in non-fiction books in your classroom or library? Have a look at different books and decide if you think the **headings** and **sub-headings** are helpful.

24 Organising writing

Organising your writing helps the reader to understand. Putting your ideas into sections helps. The simplest way to organise writing is given below.

- What happens at the beginning? (Introduce the characters.)
- What happens in the middle? (Explanation of a problem or the main part of the story.)
- What happens at the end? (The problem is resolved.)

Activity

Copy this table and sort the information depending on which question it answers. Who appears in the story? Where is it set? What is the main problem? How is it resolved? You just need to write the letter that matches the answer.

Who?	Where?	What?	How?

a) The wolf wanted to eat the three little pigs.

b) Cinderella

c) The hare slept and the tortoise won the race.

d) A straw house, a stick house and a brick house

e) Three little pigs

f) A tortoise and a hare

g) The prince found out who the shoe belonged to.

h) The wolf landed in the fire.

i) A racecourse in the woods

j) The hare boasted about how fast he was.

k) A palace

l) The girl dancing with the prince ran away and lost her shoe.

Investigate!

Can you answer these questions for your favourite story, or a story you have read recently?

25 Paragraphs

We use **paragraphs** to organise our writing so that it is easy for the reader to understand. We can group related material, or ideas, into one **paragraph**. We start a new **paragraph** when there is a change in:

- place
- time
- topic or focus.

We start a new **paragraph** by leaving a line space.

Activity 1

Copy the table and sort the phrases into those that show a change in place and those that show a change in time.

Change in place	Change in time

After that …

Back at the space station …

A few minutes later …

While they waited …

Up in the tower …

The following day …

Finally …

Further along the road …

In the classroom next door …

Activity 2

The phrases that you have just sorted can be put into sentences that start a new **paragraph**. Choose three of them to put into your own sentences.

a) _____.

b) _____.

c) _____.

Activity 3

If you were writing a recount about a holiday you have been on, you might begin with **paragraphs** about packing, the journey and arriving at your destination.

Can you do this for a holiday you have been on or somewhere you have visited?

The boxes below are an example of notes about a camping holiday. Draw three boxes with these headings and fill in your own ideas.

Paragraph 1 – Packing

feeling excited

new rucksack

checking weather forecast – choose clothes

toothbrush

Paragraph 2 – The journey

having a full car

sweets

stopping for snack

boring

arguing with my brother

Paragraph 3 – Arriving!

getting closer

spotting a sign

first sight of the campsite – adventure playground, fields, stream

wanting to make new friends

having to put up the tent

Investigate!

Can you put the ideas that you have written for each box into sentences? The sentences for each box will then form a **paragraph**.

26 Dialogue

We use **dialogue** in stories when characters are having a conversation.

Here is a conversation between Jack and his mother based on *Jack and the Beanstalk*.

The speech bubbles show what is being said here. When we use **dialogue** in a story, **inverted commas** do the job of the speech bubbles.

"What have you done, you stupid boy! Have you really sold our cow for five measly beans?"

"But mother, they're magic beans!"

We also need to explain who is speaking, as we don't always have the speech bubbles or pictures to help.

"What have you done, you stupid boy! Have you really sold our cow for five measly beans?" **said Jack's mother**.

"But mother, they're magic beans!" **said Jack**.

Activity 1

Think about how Jack's mum and Jack might speak. Choose a word for each of them to replace 'said'.

> shouted   whispered   yelled   replied   asked

Jack's mum _____

Jack _____

Activity 2

Draw speech bubbles and write your own ideas for the next part of the conversation.
Does Jack's mum believe that they're magic beans? How does Jack try to calm her down?

Activity 3

Put the words from your speech bubbles into **inverted commas**.

"_____

_____," said Jack's mum.

"_____

_____," said Jack.

27 Inverted commas

Direct speech is what the speaker actually says. **Inverted commas** go around the speech.

"If you need any help, just ask me," said Robot.

- **Direct speech** begins with a **capital letter**. A **comma** goes before the final **inverted comma** and the words that follow.

- If a question mark (?) or exclamation mark (!) are used, a **comma** isn't needed.

- Whenever there is a new speaker, start a new line.

Activity 1

Rewrite each of these sentences, putting the **inverted commas** around the **direct speech**.

a) My favourite food is a doughnut with a glass of engine oil, said Robot.

b) We like to take our robot dogs for a walk in the park, Robot's friend said.

c) I love watching *Transformers*. It's great! exclaimed Robot.

d) Where can I go to get a broken metal finger checked out? asked Robot.

e) As he watched the daleks on *Doctor Who*, Robot shrieked, They are the scariest characters I've ever seen!

Activity 2

Use the rules to help you check the punctuation in these sentences. Rewrite each one using the correct punctuation.

a) "Don't go into the cave! shouted Bilal.

b) Please can I order a burger, chips and a coke?" Joe asked politely.

c) I was thrilled to score the winning goal," the footballer said.

d) "Today will be sunny, with some showers said the weather forecaster."

Activity 3

Complete each sentence by either putting speech inside the **inverted commas** or saying who has spoken.

a) "I am going to put a spell on you!" _____.

b) "_____?" asked the teacher.

c) "We've finally reached the top of the mountain!" _____.

d) "_____," said the princess.

e) "_____!" exclaimed the giant.

f) "_____," explained the little alien.

Activity 4

Which of these sentences has **inverted commas** in the correct place?
Rewrite the correct sentence carefully in your book.

"I'm looking forward to my holiday, said the little girl."

I'm looking forward to my holiday, "said the little girl."

"I'm looking forward to my holiday," said the little girl.

"I'm looking forward to my holiday, said" the little girl.

Investigate!

What do your favourite film or television characters say? Practise using **inverted commas** by writing conversations between them.

28 Terminology check

You've been practising terminology (special words) from Year 2 and new terminology for Year 3. Let's see what you can remember. If there's anything you're unsure about, you can have a look back through this book!

Activity 1

Match each word with its meaning.

conjunction	a word that adds information to the verb
adverb	a naming word
preposition	an action or being word
noun	a word that links clauses or ideas
adjective	a word that shows a relationship of time, place or cause
verb	a describing word

Activity 2

Choose a word that is an example of each of the word classes. Add a word of your own to each word class.

because   under   television   soon   powerful   marching

a) noun

b) adjective

c) verb

d) adverb

e) conjunction

f) preposition

Activity 3

Draw each of these punctuation marks.

full stop ☐   exclamation mark ☐

question mark ☐   apostrophe ☐

comma ☐   inverted commas ☐

Activity 4

Using the examples to help you, explain what each of the underlined punctuation marks are used for.

a) The train is arriving at the station.

The first is a _____ and it is used here to show _____.

The second is a _____ and it is used to show _____.

b) I'd like a sandwich, crisps, an apple and a banana.

These are _____ and they are used for _____.

c) We are playing with John's football.

This is an _____ and it is used here to show _____.

We didn't win the cup.

This is an _____ and it is used here to show _____.

d) Where are you going?

This is a _____ and it is used to show that a sentence is a _____.

e) What fantastic weather we are having!

This is an _____ and it is can be used to show that a sentence is an _____.

Activity 5

a) Write three vowels.

_____

Write five consonants.

_____

b) Explain when you should use the determiner **a** and when you should use **an**.

_____

_____

c) Where in a word would you find a prefix?

_____

Where in a word would you find a suffix?

_____

Activity 6

Complete each sentence, choosing a verb and using the correct tense.

Last week, Oliver _____ to Rome.

We're _____ a story about robots in Literacy.

I _____ always hated sprouts.

Fatima and Jade _____ jumping on the trampoline.

Investigate!

What are you confident about using now? What do you think you need to practise a little more? Write yourself a 'smiley face' list for what you can do, and a 'things to do list' for what you want to work on.